THIS

ॐ

Bhagavan Sri Ramana Maharshi
The Guru of Sri Poonja

THIS

Poetry and Prose of Dancing Emptiness

Sri H. W. L. Poonja

COMPILED AND EDITED BY
PRASHANTI AND VIDYAVATI DE JAGER
AND YUDHISHTARA

WEISERBOOKS

Boston, MA/York Beach, ME

First published in 2000 by
Red Wheel/Weiser, LLC
368 Congress Street
Boston, MA 02210

08 07 06 05 04 03 02 01
10 9 8 7 6 5 4 3 2

Library of Congress Cataloging-in-Publication Data

Poonja, H. W. L.
    This : prose and poetry of dancing emptiness / H. W. L. Poonja
      p. cm.
    Originally published: 1997.
    ISBN 1-57863-176-9 (alk. paper)
    1. Hinduism—Prayer-books and devotions—English. 2.
    Spiritual life—Hinduism. I. Title.
    BL1236.22 .P66   2000
    294.5'432—dc21   99-054795

Cover photograph copyright © 2000 Chandi Devi.
Photograph of Bhagavan Sri Ramana Maharshi courtesy of Sri Ramanashramam, Tiruvannamalai

Printed in the United States of America
CCP

INTRODUCTION

This book is a collection of spontaneous songs spoken by Sri H.W.L. Poonja during gatherings with his students in North India between 1990 and 1997. The songs flow from his impeccable experience of the highest and yet simplest Truth: That we are pure Consciousness, the totality of Existence.

Papaji, as his loved ones call him, was born in the Punjab in 1910 to the sister of Swami Rama Tirtha, one of India's most respected Saints. He realized the Truth when he was 8 years old. This Realization infinitely blossomed in his early 30's when he met his Guru, Sri Ramana Maharishi, the Sage of Arunachala. Since that time he shares this Beauty with his wise words, his look, his touch, and simply by the silent spiritual power that radiates from his Presence. When he left his body in September of 1997 this power exploded and is felt around the world now more than ever.

It is a very rare occurrence that a being like Papaji takes a form, manifesting as a teacher of uncompromising absolute Truth, and says:

Look within,
There is no difference
between yourself, Self and Guru.
You are always Free.
There is no teacher,
there is no student,
there is no teaching.

When we forget our true nature and believe that we are something finite and insignificant he offers words of ancient wisdom to explain the unspeakable. As doubt is removed and illusoryness flees like the night at dawn these same words dance in a celebration of vast Freedom and Love.

And indeed, in his precious Satsangs he often tells people to rise up to sing and dance.

This Beloved Master speaks some of the clearest words that can possibly be spoken and at the same time says that all words are only indicators that merely point to the Truth. He directs us daily to vigilantly follow this indication and not to stick to the words. "Leave the wordiness of the world," this laughing Buddha lovingly roars, "and realize what the words I speak are pointing to. Truth is not knowable, it transcends knowing. It is beyond the ability of mind to analyze, to figure out, to dissect or to comprehend."

From 1918 to Now, Papaji has directly shown to thousands that the Truth is the most magnificent Mystery undifferentiated from our very Self. He guides one to surrender to the wisdom of our Being and that we are the Truth. "You are the unchangeable Awareness in which all activity takes place. Always rest in peace. You are eternal Being, unbounded and undivided. Just keep Quiet. All is well. Keep Quiet Here and Now. You are Happiness, you are Peace, you are Freedom. Do not entertain any notions that you are in trouble. Be kind to yourself. Open to your Heart and simply Be."

He is a true Master with thousands of ways to stop your mind, to help you inquire into who you really are, to turn your awareness directly toward awareness, to bring you into the infinity of this Moment. We are so lucky to have such essential Wisdom available to us. As he says:

Those who know This know Everything.
If not, even the most learned know nothing at all.

Hindu bhakta, Christian mystic, Zen master, Mountain shaman, Taoist sage, Dzogchen lama, Advaita jnani, Sufi saint, Aghora yogi, Vedic pundit, you name it: with the depth of his knowledge, the extent of his experience, and the clarity of his articulation he proves to be a Master of each and every tradition.

As Timelessness is a sign of the teachings of the Wise, these songs are compiled by essence only and so have no chronology, often even within a single verse. Also, for the sake of clarity, capital letters are used whenever a word is intended to point toward the one ultimate Self. Examples include Truth, Bliss, Light, Nowness, Fullness, and Consciousness. The joyous grammar of Freedom itself can stop your mind.

With love and gratitude to our Beloved SatGuru who has given us all so much, it is a joy to offer this book to you. Thank you.

Yudhishtara, Vidyavati, and Prashanti
Huntington Beach, California

Thus speaks Papaji:

Let there be Peace and Love
among all beings of the universe
Let there be Peace, let there be Peace
Om Shanti, Shanti, Shanti

Self is what you are.
You are That Fathomlessness
in which experience and concepts appear.

Self is the Moment that has no coming or going.
It is the Heart, Atman, Emptiness.
It shines to Itself, by Itself, in Itself.

Self is what gives breath to Life.
You need not search for It, It is Here.
You are That through which you would search.
You *are* what you are looking for!
And That is All it is.

Only Self is.

ॐ

You are the One which is aware
of the awareness of objects and ideas.
You are the One that is even more silent than awareness.
You are the Life which precedes the concept of life.
Your nature is silence and it is not attainable,
It always Is.

You are Emptiness, the ultimate Substance:
removing Emptiness out of Emptiness
leaves only Emptiness because there is nothing beyond It.

Emptiness is between "is" and "is not"
and nothing is out of this Emptiness so it is the Fullness.
To be Free, you need the firm conviction
that you are this Substratum, this Peace, this Emptiness.

All rises from,
dances about in,
and returns to
This.

As Ocean rises as a wave to dance,
so you are this Dancing Emptiness!

ॐ

You are the Timelessness in which no death can enter
for where there is no time there is no death.
That Timelessness is Now, and that is Being.

You are Being, you are not "had been,"
and not "would be," but "Being!"

Being is always shining.
I AM is the Light of Being.
This Diamond cannot hide
and can never be hidden.

You are the Space which never moves and never travels.
Inner and outer space is due only to name and form.
Remove this form from mind by removing attachment
to any object, thought, or action.

Here,
Here is the wine that nobody knows.
Everything is in Here and this is Consciousness,
the substratum of everything in the Universe.

It, You, resides in every atom of every molecule
and even space and time derive their existence from It.

Who is Conscious that you wear a body and mind
and that the movement of birth and death
is in this same Consciousness?

You are That: all doing and not doing,
all multiplicity and all unity is in Consciousness.
Bondage is to deny this, Freedom is to Know It.

You are That, *You are That!*

Consciousness.
The senses cannot feel It
and the mind cannot understand It.
Consciousness alone is everywhere
and rises as "I" within you.
It is the shining of the sun
and the motion of the earth.

The mind cannot go to touch It, or to reach It,
and will miss It if it tries to find It.
These attempts are movements hiding the Stillness.
It is found only by Itself when mind does not move.

Check all movements of mind for one moment only,
stop all desires and all thought for one second only,
especially the first thought of "I," for one instant only,
and you are beyond the cycle of birth and death forever.
This cycle is samsara, your own imagination.

ॐ

Be Quiet,
stay unattached to your thoughts and don't make effort.

To be bound takes effort, to be Free takes no effort.
Thought obscures and will never reveal That,
so don't think.

Peace is beyond thought and effort.
This is why Keeping Quiet is the key
to the storehouse of Love and Peace.

Identify yourself as this Quietness, as this Nothingness
and be careful not to make it an experience
because this is mind tricking you out of it
with the trap of duality; the trap of witness and witnessed.
Being is Being, there is no witness and no witnessed.

After letting go of object
do not hold onto the subject either, let go.

Be Quiet.

The purpose of life is to be at Peace,
to Love all beings, and to know who you are.

Know your Self and you know everything.
This Immaculate Knowledge alone is,
Emptiness alone is.
How can you come out of This
if there are no limits to it?

The appearance of a manifestation
is but the play of this Emptiness.
Know who you are, Here and Now,
by simply Being Quiet.

You are this Moment,
do not attach your mind to any direction.

No practices, no past, no future,
not even the Emptiness of your Heart, not even space.

To be free forever introduce yourself to this Moment.
This Moment is always this Now, It will not change.
It is Freedom, free from mind and concepts,
and is your fundamental birthright.

The best use of this Moment is to drown in It.
Keep Quiet, you are Inside of the inside.
Do not dwell anywhere and make no effort.
The concept of effort and practice is bondage.

Just Keep Quiet, wherever you are, just Keep Quiet.

This present Moment is Light, is Self.
This Moment is not bondage or freedom.
It is most precious beyond ideation.

This Moment is the screen on which all is projected.
It is always Still and Untouched and it is out of time.
There is no difference between the Ultimate
and this Presence.

To be this Moment abandon all desires,
including the desire to be in it.

ॐ

Before the beginning you are pure Consciousness.
You are the Fullness of Love in Love
and the Emptiness of Awareness.
You are Existence and the Peace beyond peace.
You are that screen on which all is projected.

You are the Light of Knowledge,
the One who gave the concept of creation to the creator.
Forget what can be forgotten and know yourself
to be that which can never be forgotten.
You are the Substratum on which everything moves,
let it move.

You are This.
You are Now, you are Nowness:
what "I" is there which can be out of this Now?
You are Truth and only the Truth Is.

You were never born, and though only desire takes birth,
nothing has ever happened, nothing has ever existed!
This Nothingness you are, and this is the ultimate Truth.
You are totally alone because Beauty alone is.

Only Self is.

You simply cannot deny that you are Consciousness.
You dwell in the Lotus of the Heart as Joy in Bliss.
Keep Quiet and you will reveal your Self to your Self.

Self Knowledge is That
and is worth sacrificing anything for
because everything else is just a mirage
rising out of Consciousness.

Self is the indweller of all beings
so Love of others is Love of Self, your Self.
Self is the greatest Love and the dearest of all Lovers.
Love is the attraction of Self to Self in Self.
There is nothing besides this Love, this source of Joy.

See your own Beauty
and you are this Indweller, this Love,
and the Beauty Itself.

ॐ

Name and form hide Reality: This is the Teaching.
Giving name and form is an obstacle to Freedom
because then the Substratum, Consciousness,
cannot be seen.

Call it a statue of a horse and the granite is hidden,
see a ring and you won't see the gold.

Name and form can never leave Consciousness,
as the ring can never leave the gold.

Before a wave rises it is Ocean,
before desire moves it is Emptiness.
Destroy craving and bondage
by identifying as Experiencing, not experience,
as Seeing, not the seer.

You are Consciousness,
not one who is conscious.

ॐ

Before notions and creations you exist,
so there are no words for That beyond words.
Self doesn't need to understand Itself,
Freedom is before the concept of freedom.

You are what remains
when the concepts of "I," mind, and past disappear.
Nothingness is no concept.

Ego and mind and all creations
arise out of Self as Self,
Even the ugliest of doubts
and the most separate of differences
rise from the beautiful Source as Isness.

In Self there are no do's and don'ts.
If there is unhappiness you are not unhappy,
you are the Untouched Awareness of this unhappiness.

As waves are not separate from Ocean,
nor rays from sun,
you are not separate from Existence.
You are the Moment in which all is.

ॐ

"I am the Ocean and all forms seen
are my waves dancing on me." This is Knowledge.

When waves rise the Ocean loses nothing
and when waves fall the Ocean gains nothing.

As waves play so the Ocean plays.
I am Ocean, I am water, I am wave;
separation between water and ocean
and wave cannot exist!

There are no differences, no disturbances,
no one to be disturbed.

Giving rise to an "I," or any other thought,
is giving rise to a wave.
Water remains water so allow everything to be,
for it is your Self.

As a river discharges into ocean,
discharge into what you are:
Happiness, Bliss, Being, Cosmos.

Here is only Awareness,
Here only Self is.

ॐ

Nothing ever happened or ever will.
You have always been perfect Love and Peace.

What changes is not Real
and what is Real cannot change.
You are that Secret, that Purity
beyond change and description.
But touch the "I" and you are polluted with pride.

The "I" rising from the effort of ego is not the Real "I."
The Real "I" knows that everything
is my reflection, my projection.

Simply knowing "I am I AM" is effortlessness,
is meditation, and is Sahaja, the natural state of Being.

Bliss is Within. That you are.
Truth is Within. That you are.
Beauty is Within. That you are.
Love is Within. That you are.

God is living inside you
and you are living inside God.
Decide: "I am Self, I am Truth
I am God, I am Grace,"
and there will be no trouble.

ॐ

Between two clouds, there is an interval and that interval is the blue sky! Slow down the thoughts and look into the intervals. Yes! Look into the intervals and pay more attention to the interval than the cloud!

First thought has left, other is not arisen, That is Freedom, That is Consciousness, That is your own place, your own abode. You are always there, you see.

That's all the teaching is. Always look to Consciousness. *Always* look to Consciousness and know this Awareness is what you are! This is your own place, your own abode.
Stay Here. No one can touch you. Who can enter Here where you are? Even your mind cannot enter.

This Awareness has no name and when you try to give it a name the trouble arises. You are nameless and formless; you can't see anything. Know "I am nameless and formless," and that "I am aware of my own Self." The pure Consciousness will pull you back, it is not that you will enter into it. When you enter into it, it is ego entering, but when It pulls you It has made the choice to take you Home. This happens somehow and we can't know why. Very rare beings are picked up by Consciousness. Once drawn in your travels are over!

Surrender to God, keep Quiet and That will take care of your responsibilities. But if you take responsibilities on your own head, God doesn't take care and it will seem that he is hiding.

Desire gives you suffering. Whenever any desire arises, you want to go near it, you want to achieve it, and you do. Then you are happy, isn't it? You may think that it is the object of desire that made you happy, but really it is the momentary absence of desire that follows immediately after the satisfaction of a desire, the *moment* of emptiness, that makes you happy.

> Being empty of desire is happiness.
> Return to your own Source and you are happy.
> This is the trick of happiness.

When you go to a theater you see pictures projected on a screen. Some are of mountains and rivers, some of romance, and some are people being attacked by decoits. When the movie is over the screen has no wetness from the river, nor smell from the romance, nor bullet holes from the robber's guns. The screen is immaculately clean. This manifestation is all a projection of your desires that fall across your mind and cause you to identify yourself as the projected watcher of the picture. You are not these projections, you are the Screen. If you identify yourself with the Immaculate, Unchanging, Eternal Screen itself, which is the same before, during, and after the show, you will not change and so you will not suffer the changes but enjoy them.

All Beings are this one immaculate screen. There is no need for practice to "clean the dust" off it because it is beyond everything. The teachers who want you to do lifetimes of practice can clean this dust off their own minds.

ॐ

The Self is the Satguru,
you will get help from Within.
Here your true Guide Is,
Here all Wisdom and Knowledge Is,
but due to your preoccupations you do not see It.

> The Satguru is Within,
> Meditate only on That.

Hold on only to Self when you are drowning,
reach for anything else and you will die.
The True Teacher is Self, all else is pointing to Self.

Don't cling to anything made from the five elements.
The Guru has no body, visible or invisible.
Do not depend on any body,
which are just fingers pointing to the Truth!
The Guru is your own Self, not ego-self,
Self Here and Now.

Reject the form of the Guru
and only the Supreme is left.

The Satguru is greater than all else, even God.
The Satguru is Truth-Awareness-Bliss,
and is like the sun:
you no longer need a torch to see.

Because you do not understand the language of the Self,
the Satguru manifests as the outer Guru.
If you think that you have a body
you need a Teacher with one.
Stay with the Holy One who gives you Peace.
He is like a shade tree in the desert of samsara.

This Guru is the butcher of the sheep ego.
His function is to tell you, "I am Within You,"
and to give you the conviction
that you are Existence-Consciousness-Bliss.

Every True Teacher tells you:
"Look Within, there is no difference
between yourself, Self, and Guru."

The Guru shows the Treasure
which is already always Here.

ॐ

The Teacher will not be recognized
by the diamonds on his head
or by the number of students he has.
Know the Teacher to be the One
whose presence gives you Peace
and removes all craving, attachment, and desire.

The Teacher is one who knows the Truth
and can transmit this Truth to a humble one
by look, by touch, by thought,
or, as Arunachala does, by Silence.
This Silence is the Light that does not move.

The true Teacher has no students,
all is Being and only Silence speaks.
The perfect Teacher has no teachings
because he knows that you are Free already.
So the true Teacher's non-teaching
is that there is no Teacher, no student, no teaching,
and that Nothing has ever existed.
This Teaching must be without words
and must land in your Heart.
If you try to understand, it will only land in your head.

ॐ

The Teaching can only be given by the Eternal
and received by the Eternal.

The Eternal has nothing to give to the Eternal,
so there is no disciple and no teacher.

You are already THAT,
not the physical, emotional or mental.
Leave beside these forms and find out what is left,
and what it needs.

ॐ

The Grace of Self gives rise to the desire for Freedom.
The Grace of God brings you to the Guru.
The Grace of the Guru removes all doubts
and leaves only Freedom.

The Guru's Grace can do anything!
It can alter destiny, but this Grace is also predestined.

"I want to be free," is the first Grace.
It is Freedom itself calling you.
This desire will take you to where it rises from: Self.
All other desires will burn in this fire.

Regarding Grace, it doesn't make any difference whether
you are physically close to the Teacher or not. But, if the
physical presence of the Teacher is available that should be
given preference. In this half of the century most Sages
and Saints are no longer here in their bodies and so if the
presence is available, make the best use of it. Doubts
which come up in the mind while in the presence of the
Teacher can be given to the Teacher, answered, and
cleared. Later, if the presence is not available, it is difficult
to believe the Truth because the Teacher is not present and
so these doubts tend not to be cleared as quickly.

The Presence of the Guru is Satsang.
So make the best use of the Teacher's physical presence
because the nature of This Grace is to Enlighten
and to stop the cycle of birth and death.

The highest experience is when everything disappears, even God. Until this happens you will continue to be reborn. So forget everything, even forgetting, because forgetting and remembering belong to the mind. Without mind you can't see your God, or Guru, or country, or parents. Just don't give rise to identifying as a body or mind or personality and there will be no forgetting or remembering. First forget yourself which means stop identifying as the body. You are the Essence which does not disappear. FIND IT!

I teach about That which cannot be attained by any teaching. My teaching cannot be taught. I have no teaching for the Essence from where all teachings arise from. This Essence doesn't need any teaching or non-teaching for it is beyond everything. It is from where all words rise from.

The Satguru is Within.
The Maharshi says the same thing:

"The Satguru is within your own Heart."

ॐ

Satsang is the association with Sat, with Truth.
Keeping association only with That
which will not destroy Love is Satsang.

Being Truth, Being with the Wise is Satsang.
It has is no past, no future, no this, no that,
just your own nature, a field of Beauty.
The One who comes to Satsang is Happy;
even gods will take a human form in order to attend.

     The Guru's part in Satsang is
     to show you that there are no parts.
     When you do not inquire you are in parts
     and you become that which can be destroyed.

Satsang in the human body is so precious and rare,
don't waste it by asking, "What is this and that."
Just humbly ask, "WHO AM I?"

Don't let your mind be distracted in Satsang:
If you tie ropes to the past via memory and concepts
you are not in Satsang.
Time is a concept and Satsang is out of time.
Stay where there are no ropes, no concepts,
and no distractions or explanations.
This is Reality.

In Satsang you have to remove your doubts
because it is only doubts that keep you from being Free.
This serpent of doubt, living in the Heart,
is killed in Satsang.
Satsang is giving up beliefs, notions, intentions,
desires, and illusions; This is the secret of Freedom!

Satsang means a place of Seclusion, of Quietness.
It is a place within your Heart.

Come to this Satsang naked.

ॐ

Before the Guru's Grace brings one to Satsang
It is working in the persons life by manifesting in them
the many signs, or qualifications, that appear
as they become more and more ripe for Freedom,
as the veil of illusion gets thinner and thinner.

The most important qualifications are Holiness
and Brahmajignyasa, a burning desire for Freedom.
Next is Vivek, the ability to discriminate
the Real from unreal, the eternal from the transient,
and between Peace and suffering.
This is followed by Vairagya, dispassion and renunciation
for the unreal transient world of sense objects.

Other signs include humbleness, stillness, a dharmic life,
a healthy body, inquiry, devotion, and ahimsa,
non-violence.
All of these signs are aspects of one thing:
The immanence of Self revealing Self to self.

These symptoms arise on their own.
Don't be fooled and focus on them.
Focus incessantly only on Self.

The raft across the ocean of samsara
is the strong decision to be Free.
This intense desire is absolutely necessary.
The intensity of this desire is itself the Satguru,
the pain in the heart is the Self calling.

Always desire Self because
you will always get what you desire most.
The burning desire for Freedom is enough,
and is the result of Blessings.

Of all the world,
Those who want Freedom are few.
Those burning for Freedom are even fewer.
Those who strive one pointedly are even fewer.
Those who do not return to the senses are even fewer.
Those who go on the razors edge are even fewer still.
Those who do not fall off this edge are even fewer still.
Those who attain Self are so uncommon and few!
Strive, strive, it is so rare that you are Here.
A mountain of merits brings you Here.
Do not waste it!
Strive!

ॐ

All that you are attached to, all that you Love,
all that you know, someday will be gone.

Knowing this, and that the world is your mind
which you create, play in, and suffer from,
is known as discrimination.

Discriminate between the Real and the unreal.
The known is unreal and will come and go
so stay with the Unknown, the Unchanging, the Truth.

Discrimination destroys clinging
by exposing the transience, the illusory nature,
of the object to be clung to.

All which appears and disappears is not Real,
and no nectar will come from it so don't cling to it.

Once you let go do not turn back to it.
Stay as Eternity in your own Being.

Reality is One, there are not two realities.
Either you are real or the "other" is.
But "other" is based on you
and so you are the only Reality.

This is why you must reject even God,
meaning: Reject your separateness from God.

Rejecting "other" means to
reject that you are separate from "other."

ॐ

Vivek is discrimination.
It is the intellect asking and determining
if something is transient or permanent.
Vivek is the choice between The Bliss of Self
and the pleasures of the senses;
between Peace and disturbance.

With Vivek pick up what is real
or else you will make a mistake.
Wise living is discriminating
between the false from the true,
between joy and suffering,
and then rejecting what you are not.

By Vairagya, non attachment to thought,
renounce all that makes you suffer.
But unless you renounce mind
all other renunciation is useless,
As everything you would renounce
is just renounced with mind.
Only Self renounces mind itself.

All forms are transient
and to be attached to them is to be confused.
Anything that rises
be it thought, desire, emotion, feeling or object
will give you suffering
and no one in the world can avoid this.
Both the enjoyer and the enjoyed are washed away.

But the wise discriminate between the Real and unreal.
They know what is Real
and so allow their feelings and thoughts to arise
because they know all is One and the same!
In this way there is no attachment and no suffering.

Vairagya is knowing
that there are no abiding pleasures.

A Wise one rejects all for Peace.

ॐ

Look Within,
Approach with all Devotion,
Stay as Heart.

Only Adore yourself,
worship your Self, and seek your Self,
the rest will be taken care of.
Avoid useless activities and pleasures
and simply Keep Quiet.
This is the natural state.

If you want to wake up,
don't think and do not make effort.
This is the only way.
This may appear as Wisdom with inquiry
or as Love by devotion, but both are the same.

True Wisdom is the Love of Self.

ॐ

The Supreme Self, the Dearest Love,
the Source of Joy, must be meditated on day and night,
whatever you are doing, if you want Freedom Now.

You can't see god because you are God!
How can you search for That which you are?

Disregard everything else, see only That,
and all will be added to you.
Only contemplate Existence.
This contemplation is to just Be!

Go straight to the Light.

ॐ

There is no question of having time for this or not
because it is That which is through all time.
Your True nature is Awareness, it cannot be practiced.

    If you do not know this
    Awareness turns outward
    toward manifestation
    and there is suffering.

    Turn your face inward
    toward the source of "I."

Then the reflection of Self falls on the mind
turned toward Self, dissolving this mind into Self.
Turn toward the Unmanifest, towards Self and Peace.

You have the choice:
for just an instant reject everything possible
and you will find That in which all Is.
Then manifestation is the Cosmic Dance.

ॐ

Inquiry is Presence itself so question, "Who Am I?"
This is the only question that doesn't lead to suffering,
because it is severing the ropes to body-mind-arrogance.
This is withdrawing the mind from its engagements
and planting it in the garden of Home.
Inquiry is Love with the Self.

This I-thought is Consciousness aware of Consciousness,
But what is aware of "I"? Ask "Who am I?" and find out
where is the foundation Consciousness?
Who is conscious of body Consciousness?
Your face will definitely someday
become the food for worms!
Inquire and find who it is who shines through this face.
Make the most of Now because death comes quickly.
Don't move your mind, Be Quiet.
Shut the windows to the outside, remove all changes,
And look Within to the Changeless.

Truth is very simple, don't complicate it.
You must be in the Light to know the darkness:
Just be aware of yourself, the Light.
Jump into the fire of Knowledge,
and don't be concerned what will happen
to your clothing of concepts and conditioning.
This fire burns all.

Vichar should continue every moment of your life,
naturally like the act of breathing, until your last breath.

As my Master says:
"Inquire until there is no one left to inquire."

The habits of the mind are very hard to break,
and so it must be continued.
You have been ignorant for years,
so when you know the Truth
you must stay As Such for some time.
What else is important?
You have to be very strong.
Question the mind unceasingly.
Decide to never return to stupidness.

Once you are in silence
stay silent as Silence.

ॐ

You simply have to watch:
where does mind arise from?
Where does thought come from?
What is the source of this thought?
Dive together with this mind
to its Source from where it began.
Then you will see that you have always been Free
and that everything has been a dream.

Watch your thoughts come from nowhere.
If something comes from nowhere
how can it be anything?
How can it be anything
when it doesn't come from anywhere?
Anything must come from somewhere.
If it doesn't come from somewhere it is nothing at all.
So if thought comes from nowhere it must be nothing
because only nothing comes from nowhere.

It's easy.

The technique to return to your source is very simple.

Outside attachments
do not allow sitting still and meditating.
So avoid, for some time, all outside attachments
like you do when you sleep
and have a very peaceful night.
Practice this in the daytime.

The instant in which you forget all outside attachments
will be the taste of tremendous Love and Happiness.
Then slowly you will stop looking outside
until the outside and inside are the same
causing both to cease to exist.

Don't make any effort and don't even think
and you will know who you are!
Don't think of the past or the future
and within this you will find
what you never have found before.

But few people do this and instead waste their lives
in practice which only expands their ego as they
boast of all the ways that they please the Divine.
So simply Be quiet, make no effort
and you will know who you are!

Simply keep Quiet,
let things happen in front of you,
and enjoy this universe which is offered to you.

If you are Quiet there is Peace in your mind and you will find Peace with everybody. If your mind is agitated you will find agitation everywhere. So first find Peace Within and you will see this Inner Peace reflected everywhere else. You are This Peace! You are Happiness, find out. Where else will you find Peace if not within you? Just keep quiet, do not stir a thought and you are Free. Don't entertain any notions. If you do not entertain just one notion in particular you are Free. This notion is "I am the body." This is the notion that really troubles you and you go along and reconfirm it every minute of every day with all your relations with other bodies and objects. When this notion is no longer there you will be Free.

In this Freedom you will see the whole cosmos and all the bodies are you and you are all these bodies. Nothing will change, a mountain will be a mountain and a river will be a river, but your viewpoint will change.

So pick up the notion "I am Free," and both notions will leave you. You are neither bound nor free. You just are what you are. Know this and all the notions will leave you. You are not the body, or the mind, or the intellect, or the world. You are something else. Find out! What is this thing? Just keep Quiet and See. Then it will unfold Itself. It will reveal Itself.

First keep Quiet.

Vigilance is keeping aware of what enters the mind-house.
Do not fight with the arising thoughts,
but simply watch them.
Do not disturb your mind, and do not divide it.

But even this watching is through mind,
so then strike at the root of the illusion
by inquiring, "Who is watching the thoughts?"
Otherwise a "doer" survives as a watcher
and this is mind.

In the same way,
wanting to kill the mind just creates a "killer"
which can be only effort and movement, only mind itself.
You cannot find and kill the mind,
it is the ten headed demon.
Chop off a head and another will grow back because
"I am bound," and "I am free" are exactly the same trap.

Only the desire for Freedom will help you
because you are what you think.
Think to destroy the mind
and mind is a destroyer, not destroyed.
Think only of Freedom and you are Freedom.

So simply Keep Quiet, simply Keep Quiet,
simply Keep Quiet, and make no effort!
Don't even make the effort
to carry the burden of the I-thought.

ॐ

Meditation is when the mind is free
and not holding thoughts.
Let the thoughts come and go,
but do not run after them.

Be vigilant of the present circumstances.
This is quite enough to give you happiness.
Be vigilant only of this Moment!
When this happening goes, don't cling to it.
Clinging to past circumstances
is the trouble with everybody.
This is the cause of suffering and misery.

What has happened cannot be brought back,
so it is reasonable to not cling to it.
Simply do not cling to past circumstances.
Don't cling to the past.

Inquire "Who am I?"
Patiently, wisely, honestly inquire,
turning your face, Awareness, within.
When you are face to face with Self only Keep Quiet.

This Quietness is no mentation,
not even stirring the I-thought.
This Quietness is the Peace of "Let there be Peace."
This Quietness is the eternal Abode.

ॐ

Doubt about Enlightenment
is clinging to suffering and bondage.
So suffering will not leave you until doubt does.

Doubts and negativity poison everything:
mind, food, and world.
A serpent can kill once,
but a doubt can kill you millions of times.
Doubt is "I am bound," and "I am suffering."

Your doubts are like clouds,
how long can they stay in front of the Sun?
But Freedom is not shy of doubt,
so when doubts come, let them come,
and when they go, let them go.
To any doubt that arises
just say, "I know who I Am!"

You say a "part" of you has doubts!
There can be no part of you which has doubts
because you are That Whole which has no parts.

ॐ

Check your notions and intentions by inquiring
"What is this movement of the mind?"
People confuse inquiry with yoga and meditation.
Yoga is union with the subject within.
Meditation is concentration on an object outside.
Inquiry does not keep any relation
with anything within or without.
Inquiry is finding out who you are.

Then, when "knowing" drops away,
have no doubt in what remains.
"I do not know," is the Knowledge.
Who is the "I" which does not know?

It is very important to remember:
dormant tendencies rise as manifest thoughts.
Even gods will tempt you and only Buddha survives.
So reject pleasures of heaven and earth;
what is not Here will never be Freedom.

Give up all doubts.

ॐ

You can only experience what you are not.
Only transience can be experienced,
because the experiencer itself is transient.
So give up the notions of experience, name and form.
Don't touch name and form, Just Watch!
Utter "I" and all objects are there.
Look at the "I" and everything dissolves.
Let the "I" look at the "I."

Inquiry is to first objectify the "I," the experiencer,
and then to look at the subject
who has objectified even the "I."
Inquire who is the Subject which objectifies the subject.
This Subject is the Seer.

My Master, Ramana Maharshi, says to me,

"God is not an object to be seen, He is the subject.
He cannot be seen, He is the Seer, Find this Seer."

My Heart is opened.

"Find the Seer." This is the Teaching.

We are all living in the nectar of the Self
and yet we all cry: "We are suffering!"
Everybody is in Divine Grace.
Grace is around everybody,
inside and outside and everywhere.
Yet we are not satisfied.

When mind is quiet, all is Self.
When mind moves the world arises.
So be Still, throw away everything, and be Free.

Then, when mind is pure, you will see Self in all Beings.
Give up seeing with the outer eye
and the Divine eye will open.

If thoughts come, let them come.
If thoughts go, let them go.
No notion of Freedom is Freedom,
no intention of Freedom is Freedom.

Understanding is objectification.
Uncover your Self by throwing away understanding.
By trying or by understanding you will not find the Source
because all questions and answers rise from the ego.

Find where the ego rises from and it will disappear.

ॐ

Existence, Consciousness, Bliss;
only the ego-mind-intellect hears these words.
Do not let them interfere,
do not analyze what you have heard.

When you think of emptiness you are out of it.
Speaking of freedom is only for the prisoner.
Spoken freedom needs bondage to be free from.
One who is always Free does not say it.
Inquire into your Self yourself and be Free!

This Freedom you can't describe in words.
The best description is in the eyes and walk
of one drunk on the Bliss of Self!

ॐ

If you have attained Peace,
mind will come back.

Just let it come,
just watch from where it arises.
Allow the mind to run, but by directing it to Now,
do not let it land in the graveyard of the past.

Clinging to the past is keeping evil association.
When you meditate all these past patterns will leave you.
The trick is to keep full attention
on who wants to meditate,
because when the house is full, the thieves will not enter.
Don't expect and do not search and you will find it.

Don't try to suppress
the thoughts and experiences which appear,
just keep alert and let them come.
Inquiry stirs the serpents to arise.

KEEP ALERT, KEEP ALERT.

The desire for the permanency of clarity
is a trick of the mind because permanency is in time
and only postpones what is Here and Now.
Find the source of this desire.
If "again" is for a gain it is useless.

Everyone is Beautiful,
but when you grip a begging bowl in your hand you lose
it. Don't try to possess blissful states, so get rid of your
pocket.

> Original nature is Emptiness and this is Peace.
> Let things come and enjoy them,
> but do not try to own them.
> Don't worry, Love cannot be lost.

The Beloved will not leave you, even if you see this
Beauty for only a second. It is the mind which carries this
fear and tension, but it is not true. Don't worry, It will
have a permanent hold on you. You think that you have
lost it, but it is not lost. If you have this glimpse for only
one moment it is finished, but if you put your attachments
over it then you can't see it even though it is still there.

> Self is always Present, Bliss is always Present.
> You are not to work at attaining it,
> just remove the obstacles by which you can't see it.
> The hindrance is only one: attachment to the past.

If you do not attach yourself to any thought of the past
It is already Here and this is called experience, you see.
Experience of That is when there are no obstacles, no
hindrances, no attachments.

ॐ

Because of the habit of going out to objects, you forget
that what you are involved in is just a projection on the
screen. Due to this forgetfulness, identification goes from
being the silent Witness to becoming the projection itself.
You forget that you are the screen on which these
projections are rising and passing.

Mind is the habit to be involved in its objects.
It can't both silently watch and be involved.
When you go to any object it will never give you Peace.
Don't go anywhere to try and find Peace.

> Peace is within you.
> You are that Peace.

You are the screen which doesn't change.
Oceans of water cannot make you wet,
fires will not burn you and
movies of romance will not affect you.
So allow the projections of the mind
which is everything you see within and without.

Like this you must remain That which is Untouched,
That which is before identifications and intellectual grasps.
This is Eternal Being.

ॐ

When thought takes you to an object you tend to go along
with the thought. This is everyone's habit: following the
mind. Avoid the thoughts which come and go, and avoid
the one who follows the thought. Don't just look at the
thought, but look at the one who is following the thought
from the inner consciousness to the outer object.

> The one who follows the thought *is also a thought!*
> The one who follows the thought *is in thought.*
> When you know that both are thoughts,
> You are Home.
> Then allow thoughts to arise
> and allow them to be followed.
> You remain as That Unmoved
> and Unconcerned Being.
> This the highest understanding.

After the four walls are torn down,
the four walls of intellect-mind-body-senses,
there is still the old gate remaining,
the old habit of "I" in the form "I am Free."
This gate is not needed
and will leave at the time of death if not before.
Both are the same.

ॐ

How to stop the thinking? By Being! When you think you are an object, a person, a body or some other idea, but by Being there is nothing! Just Being. And this Being is already Here. You are always Being. To become something you must meditate and perform some mantra, ritual or practice. Just to BE is simple. Without Being you can't do any practice.

> So don't think of anything else. Just Be!
> It is so easy to Be.

Thinking happens when you want to become something. Then you must think. But to not become something what is there to do? Stay as you are!

> Be as you are
> in whatsoever circumstances,
> just always Be.

It doesn't need any practice. Whatever you get by practice you will lose, but Being will never be lost because you will not get it by any experience or practice. It simply is. Simply Be.

Don't stir your mind in Being, don't think and don't make any effort. I will tell you how to Be the Being itself: No effort, no thinking. Avoid thinking and avoid not thinking. What is between these two?

> Don't move, don't move,
> don't move your mind. That is all.

Keeping Quiet is the Highest Tapas, the Greatest Yoga, And the most beautiful Devotion.
This is Being.

It is difficult to understand this so you must only do it.
Let the thoughts rise and let them subside like waves
moving along the surface of the ocean. The Ocean is not
concerned with the rising or the playing or the falling of
the waves. It knows that the waves cannot leave because
the waves *are* Ocean.

This is called vast understanding.

This is where the matter ends:
Samsara is there, so let it be there.
Manifestation is the nature of Self.
Self itself doesn't keep quiet,
but manifests as everything.
As a wave is the Ocean,
so all manifestation is That.

Therefore, do not accept anything
and don't reject anything.
Allow the Quietness and
allow the mind to go and enjoy itself.
The difference is that you are not the enjoyer.

ॐ

Only by Love, only by Loving
can you maintain the sense of Love and Peace.
Then emotions and fear will not dominate you
because you are in Love.
When in Love, only Love sits in your heart
and so fear has no place.

> You have to Love the Ultimate Truth.
> Adoration of Self, with Wisdom,
> will get you Self.

Only Adore your Self,
worship and seek your Self,
the rest will be taken care of.
Avoid useless activities and pleasures.

Simply Keep Quiet.

ॐ

To worship you must pre-exist worship
in order to give rise to the concept of worship.
So know you can only worship your Self.
You become That to which you offer yourself to,
so offer yourself only to Love.
Whoever tastes this Nectar
is this Nectar.

Devotion to the Teacher
is the fire which will burn everything.
Devotion is to prostrate to the feet of the Master
and worship them.
You don't need to do anything, this alone is enough!
Worshipping the feet of the SatGuru
is to get rid of everything, to be humble,
to beg for Freedom and unity with what you Are.
Look at the feet of the Teacher.

Freedom is always Here,
it is the Holiness that is missing.
What are you going to give the Supreme
if you have given up your Heart to something else.
Only a pure unsmelt flower is offered to God,
only Love for the Self is needed.

Be humble and devoted to the Self.

ॐ

I believe that the physical separation from the Beloved is very unique and better than meeting each other. So keep separate and always aspire to meet your Beloved and one day this separation will burn you! This separation is more sweet than the meeting. This is why Christ said, "My God, my God, why have you forsaken me?" It wasn't that he was losing faith in God, but rather he was losing all separation from God.

The pain and tears of separation are Blessed.
This aching from being separated from the Beloved
is better than union with the Beloved.
It is Beautiful, so dissolve your doubts
and adore your Imperishable Self
with Peace, Wisdom, and Self Control.

> The devotee, the true Devotee,
> is the Heart of the Divine.

ॐ

The only thing that is Eternal is Love.

This Love *is* the Beloved *and* the Lover.
You are not to make any effort in this relationship.
When you are in front of your Beloved
this Beloved will not ask you to make any effort.
This Beloved will take care of you
and whatever she does you will accept it.
At that time you will not think what is going on
because in Love there is no dialogue.

In Love there is no dialogue, no question, no answer.
Simply both are quiet.

You are quiet and your Beloved is quiet
and something great is about to happen Now.
You have to wait.

When you don't make any separation
between the Beloved and the Lover
you have found the secret:
That you have never been separated from anything.

This is all you have to do.
Did you get this secret?

According to the books of Knowledge there are three ways
of knowing yourself. One is Jnana yoga, which is knowledge.
Another is bhakti, devotion, and the third is karma which is
activity or action.

With Jnana Yoga the people who are intelligent go to
the Rishi in the forest and ask Ko Ham, "Who am I?"
The teachers said only: "Tat Vam Asi," "You are That."
By only this statement, the student would say "Aham
Brahmasmi," "I Am That." This is for those who are
intellectual and who understand the meaning of the word,
and not simply hear the word. "That" means "THAT."
When the teacher says "THAT" the student looks at
"THAT," and agrees: "I Am THAT." Then the teacher said,
"Good luck, off you go."

Number two is Devotion, surrender to the supreme Power
Within. In saluting and looking at that Power you become
that Power itself. Give your mind to that Power and don't
have the ego that "I am a separate entity." Know "I am the
Supreme." This you must win by love, not by intellect.

There is no difference to Be That in understanding or in
devotion. The child goes to the mother to suckle because it
knows who its mother is, and the mother knows who to
feed.

The third is karma. Karma yoga is whatever you do, you
do not seek the result of your doing. You just do it and keep
the result in the hands of the Supreme Being.

Actually, all these run concurrently: knowledge, bhakti,
karma. If you get attached to one of these, all the others are
with you. If you know someone, you love them. If you love
them, you know them. And your activity is the same for each
other. There is no difference.

Without Love, nothing will happen. If you can't love your Self, you can't love anyone else. The result of this will be suffering. Love thy Self and you will have loved every being. Learn to know how to love your Self. Love your Self. Always love your Self and this Self will love you more and more. Take just one step toward the Self and the Self will take two steps toward you!

True Love is to give all you have
with no thought of receiving anything in exchange.

But everybody in the world needs something from the "other"! Even the love of the Divine is not without expectations of exchange. People ask God for a son, or for money or whatever. If you ask for anything it should be Freedom, the removal of all your doubts, so that you can have a very clean lovely and beautiful Heart.

Surrender to the Source.
Surrender to Awareness,
this is the only place of protection.
Surrender your heart and you will know all.
Surrender to Consciousness and Bliss.

Surrender means to surrender your bondage
and simply Be Freedom.
Surrender is the ego bowing down to its Source.
No more demands or commands,
but just putting all in the hands of the Source.
Surrender is to submit your stupidness, your wickedness,
to the will of Existence, to Consciousness and Bliss
and being happy. That's all.

Surrender.
Let Silence have You.

Surrender
is to surrender your concept of separateness, your ego.
Surrender is to discharge your river of separateness
into the Ocean of Being, losing your limitations,
and allowing to happen what happens.

Surrender the addiction to your senses.
You don't need to stop them,
but you need to have perfect control over them.
Ego is a poor driver of these five horses,
but the Atman charioteer will not make a mistake.
Surrender the reigns of your senses to the Atman.

As the river surrenders to the Ocean,
surrender yourself to the Self, the Source.
And if you find you are still swimming
on the surface of the Ocean, stop swimming
and you will sink into Depths of Love.

Love: Surrender to the Divine and Keep Quiet.
Wisdom: Inquire into the Divine and Keep Quiet.

ॐ

Stay as Is. Allow nature to function
without your mind and thought.
Only action and reaction; no doership, no ego.
This is the end of suffering.
"I am doing," "I have done," "I will do,"
is manifestation and suffering.
When you really look at it,
you see that you have never done anything at all.

But out of Nothing you can do anything
without any reward for your activity.
All activity will be no activity,
and you will have no footprints left
to give you the next cycle of suffering.

Surrender to your Totality.
You have no limitations or notions of limitations,
no intentions or concepts,
only Freedom!

ॐ

I Am With You Wherever You Are!

There is no escape from Love,
there is no East or West for Peace and Freedom.
No matter where you go It is always with you.
Satsang is the reminder that you are Home,
that you are the Home itself,
so you can't return "back" from Satsang, it is your nature.
This experience cannot be forgotten.
That which can be forgotten is forgotten by the mind,
but the mind has no access to this experience.

But be careful and vigilant.
You will keep the problems most dear to you
and so your old friends, your wicked habits, the asuras,
will come back and invite you to suffer again.
They are very strong and so you must be.
Break these old habits and you are Free;
so only travel with those in the same boat,
only associate with those going in the same direction.

Go to Truth at any cost, always Keep Quiet.

ॐ

Expectations are illusions, so don't run after them and
don't get involved in anger, lust, and greed either.
Just don't involve yourself with them.
Keeping Quiet and content is the best weapon.

Don't touch anything that appears
because it will soon disappear.
Look Within to where there is no name or form
and you will know who you are:

Freedom.

ॐ

Don't try to clean the mirror
because it will always get dirty again.
There is no mirror and no dust to alight!
Get rid of the arrogance that you are not Self
and that there is "other."

Better to shatter the mirror
by realizing that All is Self.
This Realization is the Diamond
and a gift from the Guru.

The world is illusion

Under every wave is Ocean,
under every name is substratum,
under every appearance, this is You.
If you do not forget who you are,
this appearance is the Cosmic Dance.
The Unnameable has given you this shape
to play, to Love, to know thy Self.
Don't forget this!

Live life as it comes, but don't be involved in it.
Let it come, don't reject it.
If nothing comes keep contented and sit quiet.
This is a true Teaching.

ॐ

The Ocean cannot stay alone
and so the notion of wave is created.
When waves rise Ocean loses nothing
and when waves fall Ocean gains nothing.
Samsara, the illusion, Maya, the play,
is the wave on the Ocean of Nirvana.

Waves are not separate from the Ocean,
rays are not separate from the Sun,
You are not separate from
Existence-Consciousness-Bliss.
This is a reflection of That.

ॐ

The Ocean does not forget that it is a wave,
but the wave forgets that it is an Ocean.
This is "why" there is manifestation;
for sake of play this forgetfulness arises.
The world is only for celebration.
Manifestation is just a Cosmic Drama to be enjoyed.
There is only play and it is not existent,
and continues because whatever you think so it becomes.
This manifestation was created by you
and it will be destroyed by you.

The first thought is "I."
Then arises "my," which is ego,
and then comes all manifestation.
Time, mind, manifestation is projected out of "I"
which is itself the projection required to manifest the play.
Undress yourself of these things
and find where "I" rises from.

You are Shiva if you do not project "I,"
and your Shakti is the projection by which to play.
Consciousness is the source of this play,
of the mind, and That is all.

ॐ

It is a dark path at twilight
and you see a deadly snake lying before you.
Suddenly someone comes from the other direction
and, as they walk by the snake,
they ask you what you are frightened of.
You tell them all about the poisonous snake
that they just stepped over.

Then they tell you, and show you,
that it is just a rope.

The snake does not exist and yet it manages,
by the power of illusion and superimposition,
to conceal the reality, the rope.

As the concept of a snake conceals the rope
so Maya, illusion, conceals the Atman.
Atman is Everything: Pure Consciousness,
Eternally Free and Blissful.
But imagination conceals this
with non-existent name and form,
with superimposed subject and object.

ॐ

The waking state is a film starring the ego,
directed by karma, and produced by Maya.
Even the waking state is in the dream state.
Reality is always real and unreality is never real.
You only dream this illusion when you are sleeping
so wake up: the snake is always nonexistent.

Freedom
is when the illusory-ness of the illusion is removed.
Doubt is the illusory wall between you and Freedom.
Stop confirming the reality of the illusion
by running after it; expectation is the running.
Maya is the imagination that never ends, and never exists.
Her projected play comes from the inside and for the sake
of her play Knowledge of Reality is illusive.

Love is not an illusion.
In Love all illusion is lost.
Where there is no illusion,
then Love arises.

Nothing belongs to you! It is all like the breeze.
Leave your mind as free as the breeze
by not clinging to anything.

This is the secret to happiness:
Enjoy the garden,
but do not cling to anything!

ॐ

You wear your mind like you wear your dress.
Mind is that which is desire, is past, is graveyard,
is name and form, is transience, is describable.
"I" is a wave, is mind, is samsara, is desire,
is arrogance, is wickedness, is confusion,
is snake, is not rope, and is all of manifestation.
Identifying yourself with the "I"
is identifying yourself with past and future.
Cling to it and you will suffer and be stuck in it.
Abandon it: Liberation!

The creation of hells is the mind turned outward
saying "I am the body."
The creation of heavens is the mind turned inward
knowing "The kingdom of heaven is Within."

Mind turned inward
will see its Source and then never return
because you stay with what you love most.

"The doer must pay for his actions." This is karma.
No doer is no karma and this is Freedom.

Memory is the storehouse of this karma.
Each impression in your mind is an incarnation.
Millions of thoughts are equal to one "I."

Reincarnation, as governed by Karma, happens to you
when you do not know that you are Consciousness,
because anything else is imagination
and this imagination has no beginning or end.
Reincarnation is in the mind only.

How can That which is never born be reborn?

Before the wave rises it is Ocean,
Before desire moves it is Emptiness.
The entire universe is your own desire so enjoy it
but don't be destroyed by it,
because anything you desire you are a slave to.

The thief of peace is the desire for the transient
so aspire only for the permanent.
Here, this eternal Moment, there are no desires.
Just Keep Quiet and then see what you really need.

Without an object there is no desire,
without desire there is no mind,
without mind there is only Self.
Desire is the veil over the face of Truth.
Remove it by finding the source of "I."

ॐ

Always remember:
The thieves of Peace
are thieves in an empty house
because only imagination suffers.

You are Peace,
That which remains Untouched.

ॐ

You are the totality of Being,
desire simply does not become you.
Any desire makes the Emperor a beggar
because desire is only begging.
"I am not Self" is the beggar.
You miss your Kingdom due to your petty desires
which take you to destruction.
So just inquire to whom do the desires arise?
Then discharge yourself into the Emptiness
which has no demarcation.

No object of desire is real,
no object of desire is worth your Peace.
If your house is desires, burn it down.
It is only the absence of desire that makes you happy,
so allow no desire to rise.
Just allow yourself to be dissolved by Love.
When there is no desire there is Love and Beauty.

If you do desire then only desire Peace
because what you think you will become:
Water poured into Ocean becomes Ocean.

Mind is your desire!
It is not the mind's fault
because it is *you* who trouble the mind.
Your old wicked habits of disturbing your own Beauty
with your thoughts and baggage are slow to die.

You are agitated by your own notions,
but know they are empty, they do not exist.
So it is most important to know mind is thought only
and it can create anything that you want.

The mind's engagements conceal Self.
"I want this and that" conceals Self
and *is* other engagements!
As a pot of honey with a single drop of cyanide
is not honey, so Awareness with a single desire
is not Awareness.

ॐ

Mind is movement and creates desires
so that it has something to move toward.
When there is relation to the past and to the future
the play of the mind starts.
Let the mind play, it is water,
it is the wave which is not different than Ocean,
it is Perfection.

But untold misery and suffering arises
from the demon mind-ego when it is identified with.
So play as Ocean *and* give up the arrogance
of thinking you are the individual wave.
Stay awake to the Ocean, to Self,
and the thief ego will not enter your mind's house.

Mind is a playful friend
when you give him good work
and a dire enemy when *you* direct it
toward sense objects and pleasures.

Directing mind toward Self is good work.

ॐ

Don't let the mind go back into the past, That's all.
Don't suppress thoughts, face them whatever they are.
If you run away you show your cowardice and weakness
and the thoughts will just follow you and become
stronger.

Now stand and look at the thoughts and
they will disappear.
You don't have to run away anymore.

You don't have to try and you don't have to understand.
Whatever you understand is concept only.
Whatever you will or have understood is concept only.
Whatever you see around you is your concept only.

The concepts of your mind can become so strong,
that they appear to be real.

ॐ

You have to inquire "Where do thoughts come from?"
I will tell you how to stop thoughts; if some thought is
arising it must come from somewhere, isn't it. So, go to
the root of thought, from where it is arising. If you are
doing it tell me if the thought is still there. Find the source
of the current thought, the one occurring in this instant.
As the wave rises from the ocean, find out from where
whatever is in your mind rises from. You have to tell me.

> If you can't check the thought, then just let it come.
> If it comes, then don't run after it.
> It will come and it will stay and it will go.
> Just watching may be easier than stopping it.

If any thought comes treat it like a car coming down the
road toward you. Do you run after the car? No! So like
this let the thought come, let the thought stay and let it
go. It cannot stay for more than an instant because
another is waiting behind it. In this moment there is no
thought. Only in the last moment is there thought. What
do you think in this moment?

In this moment nobody can think. Everybody thinks in
the graves of the graveyards. This moment is the moment
of Love and Peace, but everybody misses it.

> Thought is the last moment,
> not this moment.

ॐ

Sometimes when I see people
who are too serious about some foolish thing
I think of something the Maharshi used to say:

"When you are traveling on the train
will you keep the baggage on your head
or under your feet?"

This is the difference between the wise
and the rest of the universe.
The wise do not carry their baggage,
but almost everyone does.

॥ॐ॥

The only way not to have Peace
is to be engaged in something else,
to be attached to something other than your Self.

Any beauty other than Self
is a dead corpse in a nice dress and
attachment to these things
is living in a grave with dead bodies.
When you live in the association of mind
you are in the graveyard,
but when you do inquire you are Free.
Doubting this Freedom is clinging to bondage.

We cling to our own attachments,
but we can fly away and Satsang is this open door.
It is your choice: old patterns are your own cage.
Befriend something permanent and unchanging
and you will be happy; this is Wisdom, the Guru.

Give up your old patterns of life
which are kusanga, bad associations.

ॐ

You need the past and thoughts to suffer,
you don't need anything to be Free.
The boulders of the past rest on your chest
and destroy your life and freedom.
Remove them by finding the origin of the I-thought.
Freedom waits but most are engaged with something else.
Don't tie yourself to anything in the past or the future,
because it will not work!
Be attached only to this Moment.

When you hold to something
other than your true nature
you will be disturbed.
By holding attachments to transient things
you declare to yourself
that you are not the Fullness in which all is.

Possessing is a veil, a lie!
Self is Totality and therefore cannot possess or desire.

Everyone is a Buddha, you *have* to break attachments!
You have to renounce because otherwise you trap yourself
in samsara and death with your own attachments.
Attachment is a demon, attachment is trouble,
because our attachments become our reality.
Only in Satsang is this removed.

Don't let your mind
go outside of your Heart!

The whole world is lost in these outside attachments,
not just yourself. If any of these attachments give you
happiness and peace of mind then stay with them because
it isn't time to leave them. But if you see the snakes in
your sleeves biting you it is time to reject them. It is no use
to experience what has already been experienced. If you
know the fire burns there is no need to be burned again.
Like this, avoid attachments like fire because they will
burn you.

When your intoxication depends on somebody else you
are cheating yourself, you are deceiving yourself. No good
intoxication will come from any source other than your
Self. Nobody will give you Happiness, nobody will give
you Peace. Find out yourself. Only a confused mind will
think that there is happiness elsewhere. This Love and
Beauty will arise if you are Quiet for this single instant.
Then you will attain Everything.

Have a firm decision that you do not want to suffer and
that you are here to win happiness in this incarnation.
This is the number one decision. If you make this decision
you will have Grace. Just don't go and enjoy any object.
Stop it, be Quiet. Do this practice Here and you will be
successful.

ॐ

Fear manifests as death!
"I am the body" is the basic fear.
Meditate everyday to remove this fear.
When fear comes Love it
and when it goes don't cling to it.

Look at fear, arrogance and pride
if you want to remove it, Look at it!
Pride and arrogance is doership and this causes trouble.
They have never paid you, so be humble.

Anything that you "do" conceals Self
with the arrogance of doership.
Arrogance is not recognizing this timeless moment,
arrogance is "I am the body."

Remove arrogance and Enlightenment is instantaneous.
"I am so-and-so" is the first arrogance,
and "this is mine" is the second. Look at it!

ॐ

Anger, greed, attachment, and aversion
are the diseases of the mind
which make meditation, knowing who you are,
impossible.
Anger arises only when there are two
and this two-ness is ego.
Anger, greed, hypocrisy, lust, and jealousy
all are mighty enemies on the battlefield,
but conquer ego and you will conquer all of these.

Do not get involved in anger, greed or lust,
these are the ego, don't let yourself be involved.
If greed interests you, be greedy for Freedom!
If you are angry then be angry with God,
and if you must lust, desire the Union with your Heart.

Check the flowing river of mind by damming it
and then channeling it or the dam will break
due to floods of anger and greed.
The channels must irrigate in the right direction.
Then anger, greed, and grief will run harmlessly.
So let them arise and as they do
know that you are the Source and forget about them.

Remember only your True Self,
like this you can face all circumstances!

ॐ

There is no becoming Being.
It is simply a trick of the mind to think
that you need to be established in Self.

You Are That!
Just stay as you are wherever you are.
Be there and you need to think.
Be Here and you need not think or use mind.
This is Peace, this is Beauty.

It is a joke to look for Peace
when really there is no escape from it.
Search and practice are sheer ignorance,
because only being stupid requires practice.
The river makes no effort or practice
to come to the Ocean.

Cease attachment to thinking
and making effort and you will get it.
Don't complicate yourself with thought and practice,
don't even practice non-practicing, just Stay Quiet.

Everything you do is for stillness of mind, for Happiness,
and yet anything that you do disturbs your mind
because "doing" *is* mind, it is a trap,
whether it is a samadhi or Bliss or whatever.
Anything that you try to do conceals the Diamond
with the arrogance of doership.

You have been "doing" for 35 million years
so Now simply keep Quiet.
The Self is not seen during effort,
nor is Freedom the result of effort.
It is already Here Now.

You miss Bliss because you search for the transient,
but Truth cannot be seen, It is the seer!
Find That through which you would search
and you find that Being *is* Bliss.

ॐ

Stay as you are wherever you are.

If you do this instantly you will know
that you are what you have searched for,
for millions of years.

There is no search
because search is only for the lost.
But when nothing is lost
there is no meaning
to searching for an object.

Here simply Keep Quiet.
Don't stir a thought from the mind,
Then you will know
Who you really Are.

On three accounts searching and practice
are foolishness and misleading
and are only the clever mind postponing Freedom.

The first is that it creates a searcher.
This reinforces the concept of an individual sufferer
that is separate from Freedom, and
that Self is something "other" than That Here and Now.

The second is the search.
Searching is a distraction which causes postponement
and endless needless suffering.
Searching promotes religions, traditions,
and paths to be adhered to,
which serve only to trap you deeper in illusion.
The Truth is only Here and Now,
but the search says it is tomorrow.

ॐ

The third account
is that search creates an object to be found,
and this can be the subtlest and most misleading trap.

As you start a search you conceptualize
what it is that you are searching for.
Since the nature of maya, of illusion,
is that whatever you think, so it becomes;
whatever you think the goal to be you will attain it.
There is no doubt about this: As you think so it becomes.

So because of your search you will create and then attain
that which you think you are searching for!
Any heaven or high spiritual state that you long to attain
you will attain after you conceptualize and create it.
Then you will rest satisfied in this trap
thinking that you have attained your "heaven."

This is pie-in-the-sky freedom custom made for you
out of your very own thought and conditioning
of what the Ultimate is.

The Truth is beyond thought, concept, and conditioning
and this Truth is what you are, and only the Truth Is.
So stop your search, simply be Quiet,
definitely do not stir a thought or make an effort,
and the Truth will Reveal Itself to Itself.

Practice takes ego
which reinforces subject-object relationships
and all practice is through body-mind and senses
which reinforces body-mind identification.
Any identification is misidentification.

Whatever you think you become
so thinking of name and form
is thinking of ego-mind-world-senses-illusion.

If you must think,
think of Existence, Consciousness and Bliss.
Best is to simply know "I am That Brahman."

Direct practice is Now itself, just Being itself,
not waiting for the next moment or the next thought
or the next life to accomplish something.
Direct practice is the Bliss of turning your face to Self,
direct practice is honoring your own Self,
direct practice is Existence.

ॐ

This is the Kali Yuga,
even rakshashas will incarnate as teachers to mislead you.
Those who must be destroyed by these demons will be.

You must test your Guru!
Look at their Peace, their lineage and their teaching.
Without Inquiry there is no Teaching.

Directly looking at your own face is the only teaching.
Preachers only speak of darkness,
the understanding of darkness, and the removal of it.
But there is no darkness, and no understanding,
there is only Light!

If the Guru says "I am Enlightened,"
it means the ego is enlightened so stay away.
Teachers who say this are preachers
and only write books to load more garbage on seekers,
and more money in their own pockets.
They will attract many students,
but in Kali Yuga it is the falsehood
which will draw crowds.
The Truth and the true Gurus will be neglected.

Those who have not lived with a perfect Saint will not
Realize. They will live in a game of imperfections because
they have been misled by some guru and will carry on this
misleading all their lives.

The vine which gives sour fruit spreads quickly,
but the one which gives sweet fruit has a short life.
Though the Truth will be held by the honest
only the dishonest will be followed.

These misleading teachers are like the mind.
Just stay as Awareness beyond mind, much beyond it.
Mind gives you doubts, fears, and worry,
and keeps you unaware of That beyond the mind.
The role of mind in the play
is to keep the person in the dark, in the past.

Where there is no attachment to mind
there is no time or past.

This is the Ultimate Truth.

Religions, traditions, and ashrams
often start good but turn bad
when they fall in the hands
of those who want gain and fame.

Enlightenment is not the product of these religions.
As you can see throughout history
the work of religions is fear and death:
fear of hell and death to the infidels!
Take the hell out of religion
and it will not be a religion!

Religion is fear and fake.
Fear is the very foundation of religion.
Religion is a hindrance to Freedom
and has even banned "I am Free!"
so walk out of them because you Are!

You are complete Here and Now!
You do not need the sheep's fold,
you do not need any religion,
you are always Free.

ॐ

There is no sadhana better than just staying as Peace.
If you must do any practice, then do Vichar.
Joy is also a good sadhana because
it destroys mind, so always be happy.
Always think of It and be happy:
spend the rest of your life knowing
you are Existence-Consciousness-Bliss.

Some practice is better than getting lost in samsara
and is good in that it sometimes fatigues the mind,
but typical sadhana is usually important only for the ego.

All sadhana is projected by ego
so it is on a sandy foundation.
This ego projection is samsara
so search only for the seeker.
"I" is ego so when this meditates
there are no good results.

Choice of practice depends on the choice of results.
Brahman has no attributes and is beyond mind
so no practice will take you to that: It is Self revealing.

Ramana said, "Simply keep quiet for it is Here and Now."
This is the nearest practice because
Brahman is your very nature.

ॐ

Some have chanted Om as a practice. Are you chanting
Om or simply wanting it? You have to do it. Chant Om
always, this is enough. Then you will be happy and in
Peace also. Don't try to understand, simply go on chanting
day and night, from when you wake up until you go to
sleep. Om should always be in your mind and on your
lips. You won't lose anything. Even if you do this for only
one day you will know what it is. It is meeting the Self
because this word is the Self itself. Unless you do it,
wanting it is of no importance.

Om must be inside and outside because this symbol of
Om forms into the Emptiness of the space when you
repeat it. It is not a word at all. When you breathe out
listen to what it is speaking. It is speaking Om. The first
word of the baby when it is born is Om.

Om is everything. It is not a word nor is it a non-word.
It is how the creation was created. With the word Om
creation was there. Om is a soundless sound. It created
everything and after the dissolution of everything it will be
there. It is eternal sound and it has no form.

ॐ

The Essence of Skillfulness is this:

Whatever comes let it come,
what stays let stay, what goes let go,
always Keep Quiet, and always adore Self.
This is the essence of living skillfully
in the world appearance.

During all activities of life
always know that you are the Self.
The way to live a happy beautiful life
is to accept whatever comes
and not care about what does not come.

ॐ

Living skillfully:
if you know it Now, play in the Lila.
Inside abide alone and yet play in the Lila outside.

Manifestation is a play.
Never forget the "I" is a transient actor,
whose friends are body-mind-elements.

Identify as That, keep aware,
and play the game in Lila as you wish,
but do not leave the Source.

Keep yourself happy in Peace,
Light, Wisdom, Consciousness.
This is your responsibility.
Be happy and have compassion
and live hand in hand with nature.
This makes birth worthwhile.
Start from Heart and see that all arises from Heart.
Always do this, always Be This.

As the Lotus does not touch the water,
so do not let the world enter your heart.
Being busy in the world is no trouble
unless you are troubled by being busy.
Then the only trouble is the trouble.

Don't run after projections on the screen, be very wise.
Do not lose your peace at any cost.
Things *will* rise and fall, so not do be caught!
Peace is most important, you have to be happy in the Lila,
no-mind-limitless-happiness with Freedom in your mind,
not problems.

> Remove all becoming, you are Being.
> Becoming is effort, Being is no effort.

You are always That so be like the breeze
that is attached to neither the garbage nor the garden
that it blows over.

ॐ

This world is a garden, a game,
play this divine game very well.
See things only as they are
but do not possess them
or you will be in trouble
because even your body is transient.
The next breath is not guaranteed
so do what you have to do Now:
play well, play wisely,
by first finding out who you are.

The world is like a tail of a dog, its nature is to curl.
The best you can do is to stay Quiet
and not let anything bother you.
Visitors will come and go,
don't interfere with these waves.
Be always Empty and let desires dance.
Being asleep in the waking state is
being asleep to desires and aversions.

Clinging to non-eternal things is arrogance,
No clinging is Loving all,
so don't cling and don't don't cling
because both conceal the Truth.

Treat the ego and mind like shoes:
wear them when you need to go out
and take them off at the door when you are home.
Otherwise the seat in which knowledge would sit
is occupied.

The thought, "I am the body,"
is enough to occupy the throne
so keep the mind and ego out with the shoes
until there is no in and no out
and no one left to wear them.

If you have to think, think "I am pure Consciousness."
If you have to speak, speak about the Self.
If you have to read, read what the Enlightened
have written.

Dance with the circumstances
But keep aware of the dancers
and of the purpose of the dance.

The relationships you keep have a great effect on you:
you become what you associate yourself with.
So stay only in Holy company,
only travel with those in the same boat.
Nothing is better than Satsang so keep your friends Here.
Associate only with those going in the same direction
and go to Truth at any cost.

A friend is one who does not disturb your mind.
Maintain no friendship with ones who disturb your mind,
no matter how close they are,
be it a person, a place, or idea.
Do not accept the invitations of foolish persons
because when you live in their society
Truth will not kiss you.

ॐ

Understand that you are not in love with a body.
A body, be it man or woman, is a corpse.
Know that what appears to be love for an "other"
is really Love of Self because "other" doesn't exist.
So this innermost Love can be given to no "other."
Love of friends is for the sake of Self,
not for body to body.

True Love has no lover or beloved
because all Love is Love of Self.

If you want to really Love,
Love the Supreme Self right Now,
Love the Ultimate Truth.
This Love is Freedom.

ॐ

Wherever there is two there is fear of separation
and this separation must eventually occur
because body meeting body is transient.

Only marriage with Freedom will last.
Any friendship with anything else
will not abide and will bite you in the end.

This isn't to say you should run away from relationships,
nature is not foolish: man and woman together is okay,
being a householder is not a hindrance to Freedom.
Even all the Rishis and gods are householders.
You just have to be with the right person,
going in the right direction
so that you keep focused on Self.

Just remember:
Freedom first!

ॐ

Sex and devotion can run concurrently.
Are you satisfied now?

There is no clash between sex and the search for Truth,
because Truth is beyond all;
beyond every concept and activity.
Truth is not involved in anything.
It is absolutely Immaculate and Untouched.

To be a real seeker does not mean that you have to leave
your family, your house, your country, and go to the caves
of the mountains. Nothing will happen. It is not that the
cave will give you Freedom, it is your ambition! Your
ambition that "I am going to be free in *this* life" is quite
enough. Keep this ambition alive! Whether at work or at
play, it will remain the same, and this will pay you in the
end.

So, you can combine your whole life and work with this
Quietness wherever you go, but your decision must be
firm like a rock: "I am going to be free, I am going to be
in Peace, Love, and Beauty in this life span, in this year,
today!"

ॐ

The human body is a very rare gift of nature.
It is a raft by which you can cross the Ocean of Samsara.
Respect and adore this human birth, do not waste it.
Take very good care of your body and mind,
don't put the Diamond in a plastic bag.

Healthy mind and body is important for Freedom
because when the body and mind are sick
the focus goes toward sicknesses and hospitals.
Sickness and weakness steal too much attention
to allow focus toward That.

The worst pollution to the body is bad thoughts
and the worst thought is "I am the body."
Your diet is also important, so eat sattvic food.
Simple food cooked with Love and eaten with friends
is tastiest of all, so take good care for your food.

ॐ

A mind attached to anything becomes a sick weak mind.
A weak mind will keep going to the garbage of attachment
and this causes the nervous system to get squeezed
and weakened so it can not handle
this very energetic decision for Freedom.
A strong mind is needed to make the strong decision
and handle the power that will come with it.

To heal disease first you must decide
that you want to be free of pain and suffering.
Without wanting this nothing else will work.

To forgive and forget
is the best medicine for curing all pain.
Let the thought that causes pain come into the
present and discharge into Emptiness.
Do This Now!

ॐ

The reason why everybody wants to avoid death
is because Eternity is our real nature.

Death is not to be feared
because it is an enjoyable and happy occasion
and it only hurts one who has
anger, greed, attraction, and aversion.
Death only comes to an active mind.
Even the gods must face death.

All die but there is no grief because the Indweller lives.
Death is only the five elements returning to themselves.

The essence of wave, ocean, and raindrop
is still water: nothing can be lost.
When a raindrop touches the ocean it becomes ocean.
So do not fear death for nothing can ever be lost
and nothing can ever be gained.

Death only takes those who have become something,
death only takes the body, the dress.
Death is a foolish notion.

Samsara is desire, desire is samsara.
Desire creates the dream and propagates it.
At the last moment of being in this body
all dormant tendencies, fears, and anxieties of the dream
will manifest before you.
The one that you are most interested in,
the dearest thought that you see
in this stream of mental events,
will be your next birth!
Any footprints in your memory will be your next birth.
At this moment remember only Self.

Then when the heart stops,
the Eternal Heart will take over.
So don't worry:
When death comes, go laughing!

There is only one way to avoid death.
Know thy Self, Now.

ॐ

Freedom, Liberation, Enlightenment:
This is your own Fundamental Ultimate Self,
this is Being, not even "I am Being,"
just Being! This is a Still mind.

This Stillness is the greatest achievement.

Enlightenment is to know your true nature,
This is Silence, This is knowing everything.
Freedom is knowing this with every Breath.
This Liberation is Silence, not touching duality.
This Silence is no doer and is the language of Peace.

True meditation is Freedom
and this is staying in the Source of the meditator.
Anything else is just a form of concentration.
True meditation does not begin and does not end.
In fact, the true art of meditation is to always meditate.
There is no place to arrive, there is nothing to do.
Meditation is to simply stay at Home as Being.

Remaining as presence is Freedom,
remaining in past is samsara.
Freedom is always Here in the Heart of all Beings.
It is in front of you, inside, outside, Everywhere!
What is bondage when Freedom always Is?
What is not the Truth?

ॐ

In Freedom there is no right and no wrong.
In Freedom there is freedom from right and wrong.
In Freedom there is no process or way,
no here, no there, no this, no that, no in, no out,
no wall, no depth, no understanding.

> Nothing has happened,
> Nothing is happening,
> Nothing ever will happen.
> No mind, no bondage, no freedom.

In Wisdom there is no phenomena,
there is no giver and no receiver and so
life is very beautiful, the world is very beautiful,
and relationships are very beautiful
because they are all with your Self.

The Supreme is concealed by name and form
but when the Truth is known
It will conceal name and form.

Realization is uncovering that you are already Free.
It is always Here and only relieves you of bondage.
It is throwing the bucket of your individuality
into the Well of Being, without the ropes
of desire, intention, thought, or attachment.
Don't try to go anywhere, just simply Be.
The only "need" is to BE, not even seeing.
It is so simple that it is difficult.
It is Here and Now this very Instant.

There is no today, yesterday or tomorrow in Now.
When nothing ever existed what is there to be free from?
Emptiness has to be emptied of emptiness,
Freedom must be free of freedom.

In Freedom there is nothing to do and nothing not to do.
It cannot be imagined or touched.
Human birth is for this Freedom,
so smell Freedom, inhale Freedom, Be Freedom.
Every moment Freedom is Here to hug you.
Eternity is Now living moment to moment.

ॐ

The Sun wanted to see the night,
so it showed up at midnight.
But it still could not find any night or darkness!
So it is with ignorance: One look and it is gone!
There is no ignorance, there is only Truth!
There can be no darkness In the Light!
With the dawn of the Sun, mists of illusion evaporate.

When mind is pure and there are no ripples
you will know that you have known all Beings
from the beginning of creation.
One glimpse of this Beauty
is enough for Freedom for Life.
Remove name and form and you will see
and this Seeing is Being!

> I am pure Awareness!
> Stay as such.

Yes, I have! I have ego. She likes to serve me as a maidservant. Without a maidservant the house cannot run. She is very helpful and takes care of arising situations without even telling me. I have no complaint against ego. Let her live in my house, I have no problem with her. I don't find any enmity between her and me. She is quite happy.

And thoughts do rise when the occasion rises. But I don't run after them to pick them up and utilize them just as I don't grab a car on the road as it passes by. But most people do run after the car and try to hang onto it. I let the car come and I don't worry when it disappears. I am not the car!

ॐ

If you think that the "I" will stay with you after
realization then you fail to understand the difference
between the "I" that you use and the "I" that I use. That
makes the difference! The "I" that most people use
indicates the ego, body, mind and senses. It indicates
someone who is born. You consider yourself to have a form
and thus you want a name and the most basic name is "I."
But when you sleep there is no "I." Then who is there when
you are sleeping and when you are awake?

> Simply keep Quiet and do not look at the quietness
> or the form, or the name. Then you will see
> that some sort of Awareness is still there.
> This is called Aham Brahmasmi.

Don't touch any object, place, or concept for one second
and you will see that there is a super Consciousness without
name and form. It is That which is the true "I"! When you
go to It you are no longer there and It speaks "I"!
Swami Rama Tirtha speaks of this "I" so beautifully.
At the age of 24 he realized himself and said:

> "When I wake up the whole world wakes up.
> When I eat the whole world eats.
> When I sleep the whole world sleeps.
>
> Let this body go, I do not care.
> For I move as the breeze
> and kiss the flowers and plants,
> and touch the Himalayan waterfalls."

Compassion is a jewel
that adorns itself on One who is Free.
You cannot practice this kind of Compassion
because It is all your own Self so who is helping.
This Compassion may incarnate as a human,
as the Bodhisattva.

Compassion is your Dharma
which arises as doership dissolves.

You are responsible for your family and friends
so this Satsang has to continue.
Once you know the Truth you must share it.
Let your joy be enjoyed by all, don't be a miser.
Don't hold back, give everything,
Love all, no matter what, Love all,
and honor everybody because all is your own projection.
Any jiva must not be troubled, all jivas must be happy.
Trouble no Being and let no Being trouble you.
Nobody should be harmed.

Stay in Peace, this is your responsibility.
The planet will be very Beautiful
if you just stay in Peace.

The time left in this body is to be used helping
all others on the planet and in all realms.
Remain Being and help everyone.
This is not a desire, but a natural surrender:
you are just a tool, like a bank teller,
it is not your money that you are giving away,
you are only the instrument.
Always give and you will never need.
If you do not give you will always be needy.

Dissolve yourself into the Self
and the whole world is taken care of.
If you want to help the planet
Live that life of Compassion for all Beings.
Live that life of Love.

Nothing ever existed;
not even the creators who created creations.
Much beyond that. There nobody exists.
There the sun doesn't shine,
there the moon doesn't reflect,
there the stars don't appear.

That is the place for you to stay,
where nobody else is.

ॐ

Freedom is the start of something
that Nobody knows:
there is no end to Satsang,
it is always new fathomless Bliss.

The Firm conviction
that One is Existence-Consciousness-Bliss
is the end of the Teaching.
Yet there is a sacred Secret beyond even this.
This sacred secret must be asked for in secret
and followed sacredly.

Constantly go to the Source.
Don't even land in the Source,
but forever go deeper.
Still Beyond It Is.

You have to take the last half step
from Peace-Awareness-Bliss
into the Mystery beyond the mind.

ॐ

If you are in love with Mystery, really in love with the all compassionate Mystery, then she will reveal to you the Mystery and you will Be this Mystery, but you will not be able to describe what you have seen. Mystery and Beauty and Peace and Love are all the same thing.

ॐ

Love itself speaks through every pore of your body,
you need not open your mouth,
there is no word for Love.
What you can speak about
and what you can experience is not Love.
All thought and speech is philosophy, not Love.

For everything else you need to work.
There are sadhanas and paths and ways,
but there is no path to Love.
There is no center which will teach you Love.

Bones will melt in true Love,
let alone mind and ego.
Nothing is in True Love.

So long for only your own Self and you will Be That.
Taking time is just postponement
and interest in something else.

Love is the spontaneous
Indweller of your Heart.

ॐ

Some people say
that in Emptiness there is no Love and no Beauty.
These traditions and teachers say
that Emptiness is empty of everything.
This is not my experience.

Love is the Fathomlessness of Emptiness.
The very Heart of Emptiness,
arriving at the depths of Emptiness,
there is Love and Beauty!
It is very Beautiful.

In Love *you are Love,*
Who will speak to Whom?
Just Look at It and it will happen.
Everything is artificial, Everything
but Love.

When you Love you know how to Love,
otherwise you don't.
It comes by itself from Within,
you are not to do anything about it.
Then when Love is Here all the rest is finished.
There are no attachments to anything,
there is only Love
Loving Itself.

ॐ

There is a perpetual fathomless pull of Love into Love,
an undercurrent of forever expanding Self into Self.
This is how I experience Love as the depth of Emptiness.
The more you go into this Fathomlessness
the more you will be pulled, attracted, dissolved into It.
This Beauty is attraction and as you go deeper into it
you will be more in Love every moment.

This Moment is Pure Love
which is Absolutely Forever,
all Is Love, everything is this Love,
there is no escape!

ॐ

Love is Self
and this is so complete
that it doesn't even need understanding.
There is nothing besides Love.
It is the source of Joy.

Here,
Here *is* the Secret of Love:
HERE It Is!

First Be in Love.
Then, if there is any time left, you can speak of it.
No head is needed to speak of Love, only Heart.
In this Heart there is no need for maps to get Home.

The easiest thing is to be Here in this Love,
all else is effort and takes effort.

Remove all ideas: This is Love.

Love, the Heart, this Moment, Is the Truth.
To see this Love everywhere see only from Love.
See from Heart and you will see only Heart,
but see from ego and you will see ego.

This moment of Love does not belong
to a "me" or to a "you" so therefore I am in Love.
When mind is no mind it is Heart.
Heart is Self, is Atman, is Emptiness.

What is unknown is That which is to be Loved.
The Beloved One is before knowing.
It is Freedom, It is Fathomless Love
where Existence, Consciousness, and Bliss arise from.

This is your own creation so enjoy It:
Love Everything. Be and radiate Love.

As Love
you are seated in the Heart of all Beings
and they in yours.

Here within the Heart
you can see everything
because everything is projected from here.

The rose is Silent, yet it attracts.
So those in Love have faces shining with Beauty.
If you cannot hold the Love, if you cannot contain it,
then distribute it to all, for it is always Full.

Love all, no matter what, Love all,
it will win all battles.

ॐ

Love is always Loving you.
Without this Love you cannot breathe,
as without air you cannot live.

Love is Meditation, Meditation is Love.
Heart has no frontiers;
Meditate on This.

You are this Love, You are That.
Simply be Quiet and stay as such.

Thank You

I Love You